US Citizenship Test Study Guide 2022 and 2023

Naturalization Exam Book
for all 100 USCIS Civics Questions
[Includes Detailed Content Review]

Andrew Smullen

Table of Contents

Preview

Overview

Thank you for using this study guide and congrats on becoming a U.S. citizen!

The naturalization test is an oral test. You will be asked 10 questions from a list of 100 possible questions. You must answer 6 of the 10 questions correctly to pass.

This book goes section-by-section to cover the content you need to know along with the questions and acceptable answers for each section. After that is a list of all 100 questions. The book ends with three simulated tests. Each simulated test is composed of 10 questions, selected at random from the question bank.

Important Notes

1. The answers to some questions change from time-to-time. The answers to other questions vary based on where you live. For these questions, we have provided a link and QR code that provides the current correct response(s):

studyguideteam.com/civics

2. If you are 65 years old or older and have been a legal permanent resident of the United States for 20 or more years, you may study just the questions that have been marked with an asterisk*.

Feedback

We are excited to be a part of your journey. If you have any questions or concerns, please send us an email at:

info@exampedia.org

Principles of American Democracy

Legal Documents

The National Archives in Washington, D.C., holds nearly six hundred legal documents. Among these include the Declaration of Independence, the Articles of Confederation, the Bill of Rights, and the Constitution. These documents have all been instrumental in forming the basis of the United States government.

The Constitution

> "**We the People** of the United States, in Order to form a more perfect Union, establish Justice, ensure domestic Tranquility, provide for the common defence, promote the general Welfare, and secure the Blessings of Liberty to ourselves and our Posterity, do ordain and establish this Constitution for the United States of America."
>
> - Preamble to the United States Constitution

The Constitution of the United States is the supreme law of the land, and it officially established and defined the United States government. The Constitution is important not only to the U.S. government, but to the people as well, as it lays out the rules and regulations that protect the basic rights of Americans. The rights of citizens are laid out in the Constitution's amendments.

Amendments

An **amendment** can be defined as either a change or an addition made to the Constitution, and there are **twenty-seven** amendments in total. The first ten amendments are known as the **Bill of Rights**, and they form the basic rights of American citizens.

The First Amendment states that citizens have freedom of **religion**, the right to **assemble**, the right to free **speech**, the right to **press** (journalism), and the right to **petition the government**. Freedom of religion simply means that you can freely practice any religion or no religion at all. This also means that the government cannot limit religious practices or prioritize one religion over another. The First Amendment also gives citizens the right to speak freely on any issue (in public or on paper), gather for political purposes, and ask the government to address issues.

The Second Amendment gives citizens the right to own firearms for self-defense.

The Third Amendment keeps the government from forcing citizens to shelter soldiers in their homes. During the days of the American Revolution, Americans were forced to house British soldiers. This amendment is a direct response to that oppressive measure.

The Fourth Amendment keeps the government from unlawfully searching or seizing citizens without permission given by a judge.

The Fifth Amendment ensures that citizens will be treated fairly in a court of law. It also gives citizens the right to remain silent in order to keep themselves from getting into legal trouble.

The Sixth Amendment grants citizens the right to a trial, a lawyer, and a jury if they are convicted of a crime.

The Seventh Amendment states that civil lawsuits have a right to be determined by a jury in court.

The Eighth Amendment makes sure that punishments for crimes are not cruel, unusual, or extreme.

The Ninth Amendment protects citizens' rights that are not specifically mentioned by the Constitution.

The Tenth Amendment states that any power not given to the federal government belongs to the states and the people.

Declaration of Independence

> "We hold these truths to be self-evident, that all men are created equal, that they are endowed by their Creator with certain unalienable Rights, that among these are **Life, Liberty, and the pursuit of Happiness**."

> – Preamble to the Declaration of Independence

The Declaration of Independence is the most defining American document ever written. Approved by the Continental Congress on July 4, 1776, it served as the thirteen colonies' declaration they were no longer under the sovereignty of Great Britain and that the United States of America was a free, independent nation. Though a group of five men—Thomas Jefferson, Benjamin Franklin, John Adams, Robert Livingston, and Roger Sherman—worked together to create and edit the document, Thomas Jefferson is credited as the primary author.

Fifty-six men signed the Declaration of Independence. The signing of the declaration was an act of treason against Great Britain, and doing so revealed the determination that the signers had in their desire for independence.

Governing Principles

There are seven principles of governance, as stated in the U.S. Constitution:

- popular sovereignty
- checks and balances
- separation of powers
- federalism
- republicanism
- individual rights
- limited government

Rule of law is the concept that no one is above the law and that all citizens, regardless of their status in society, must obey it. These seven principles create the backbone of the rules and beliefs of the American people and serve to define how the government should operate in the best interest of its citizens.

Liberty

Thomas Jefferson and the Founding Fathers were all influenced by the writing and teaching of English philosopher John Locke, who emphasized the ideas of liberty and equality and argued that people should be able to govern themselves without being under the control of a monarch. The Founding Fathers used these ideas to form the governing principles of the United States.

Economy

The United States adheres to two forms of economies: capitalist and market. A **capitalist economy** is one where businesses or individuals own and control most of the property and can control market prices in order to best serve the needs of society and the general public. This type of economy enables individuals to make economic choices that benefit themselves rather than give in to the desires or pressures of society. The defining aspect of capitalism is that it gives people the power to dictate their own finances and profits rather than have the state do so.

Principles of American Democracy Questions

1. What is the supreme law of the land?

2. What does the Constitution do?

3. The idea of self-government is in the first three words of the Constitution. What are these words?

4. What is an amendment?

5. What do we call the first ten amendments to the Constitution?

6. What is <u>one</u> right or freedom from the First Amendment?*

7. How many amendments does the Constitution have?

8. What did the Declaration of Independence do?

9. What are <u>two</u> rights in the Declaration of Independence?

10. What is freedom of religion?

11. What is the economic system in the United States?*

12. What is the "rule of law"?

Answers

1. What is the supreme law of the land?
   - the Constitution

2. What does the Constitution do?
   - sets up the government
   - defines the government
   - protects basic rights of Americans

3. The idea of self-government is in the first three words of the Constitution. What are these words?
   - We the People

4. What is an amendment?
   - a change (to the Constitution)
   - an addition (to the Constitution)

5. What do we call the first ten amendments to the Constitution?
   - the Bill of Rights

6. What is one right or freedom from the First Amendment?*
   - speech
   - religion
   - assembly
   - press
   - petition the government

7. How many amendments does the Constitution have?
   - twenty-seven (27)

8. What did the Declaration of Independence do?
   - announced our independence (from Great Britain)
   - declared our independence (from Great Britain)
   - said that the United States is free (from Great Britain)

9. What are <u>two</u> rights in the Declaration of Independence?
- life
- liberty
- pursuit of happiness

10. What is freedom of religion?
- You can practice any religion, or not practice a religion.

11. What is the economic system in the United States?*
- capitalist economy
- market economy

12. What is the "rule of law"?
- Everyone must follow the law.
- Leaders must obey the law.
- Government must obey the law.
- No one is above the law.

System of Government

Branches of Government

Principles
The U.S. Constitution divides the government into three different branches: Executive, Legislative, and Judicial. To ensure that no branch becomes too powerful, each branch of government can respond to and change the actions of the others. This term is referred to as the system of **checks and balances** or the **separation of powers**.

Executive Branch
The **Executive branch** consists of the President, Vice President, and Cabinet, and it is responsible for carrying out the laws of the nation. As the head of state, head of government, and **Commander in Chief** of the U.S. military, the President presides over the Executive branch. The President also has the power to veto bills or sign them into law. U.S. presidents are elected every **four years,** and citizens vote for the president on the Tuesday after the first Monday of **November**.

The **Vice President**'s primary job is to be ready to take over the presidency if the current president can no longer serve due to resignation, death, or any other reason. If the Vice President is unable to take over the presidency, then the **Speaker of the House** will become President. The President's Cabinet has many different responsibilities, along with advising the President and overseeing the everyday management of federal laws. The **Cabinet**-level positions include:

- Secretary of Defense
- Secretary of State
- Secretary of the Treasury
- Secretary of Commerce
- Secretary of Education
- Secretary of Energy
- Secretary of Homeland Security
- Secretary of Labor

- Secretary of Veteran Affairs
- Secretary of Housing and Urban Development
- Secretary of Health and Human Services
- Secretary of the Interior
- Secretary of Transportation
- Attorney General

Legislative Branch

The **Legislative branch** includes the **Senate** and **House of Representatives**, which together are known as **Congress**. In the Senate, there are two senators that represent each state. In the House of Representatives, each member represents an individual district, and some states have more representatives because they have larger populations than other states. There are **100 Senators** and **435 voting members in the House**. Senators are elected to serve for **six years** while Representatives are elected every **two years**. This branch is responsible for creating the federal laws that govern the American people and government officials.

Judicial Branch

The **Judicial branch** consists of the **federal courts**, which includes the U.S. Supreme Court. The **Supreme Court** is the highest court in the nation, and its **nine justices** are appointed by the President and confirmed by the Senate. The number of justices is determined by Congress. The Judicial branch is responsible for reviewing and explaining laws, resolving disputes, and deciding if laws go against the Constitution.

Governmental Authorities

Under the Constitution, there are some powers that specifically belong to the federal government and some that belong to the states. Some of the federal government's powers include printing money, declaring war, creating an army, and making treaties. The states have more local powers such as providing schooling and education, providing protection through law enforcement agencies, providing safety through agencies such as fire departments, granting driver's licenses to qualifying citizens, and approving zoning and the use of land.

Federal Agencies

Federal agencies are government organizations that hold specific powers that help them regulate industries and take care of national issues. Though there are many agencies, some include the U.S. Department of Health and Human Services, the U.S. Environmental Protection Agency, the U.S. Federal Reserve, and the Federal Bureau of Investigation (FBI).

Local Agencies

Local agencies are organizations that help care for and provide everyday amenities and services. Some local agencies include law enforcement services, county libraries, public education systems, wildlife conservation agencies, historical preservation commissions, transportation agencies, and waste management services.

Who Represents You

Parties

There are many parties in the U.S. political system, but the two most prominent and powerful are the Republican and Democrat parties. Other parties include the Libertarian Party, the Green Party, and the Constitution Party.

The **Republican Party** started in 1854 and is generally conservative in political views. Republicans advocate for less government control in the economy and for economic and social independence. Some notable Republican presidents include Abraham Lincoln, Theodore Roosevelt, Ronald Reagan, and George W. Bush.

The **Democratic Party** started in 1828 and is generally liberal in political views. Democrats advocate for more government regulation of the economy and for economic and social equality. Some notable Democratic presidents include Franklin D. Roosevelt, John F. Kennedy, Jimmy Carter, and Bill Clinton.

Federal Officials

Federal officials are individuals who serve at the federal level. These include the President, Vice President, senators, and representatives.

State Officials

State officials are members of a state's government. They include the **governor**, lieutenant governor, attorney general, state justices, and state judges.

To find who represents you, go to studyguideteam.com/civics or scan the QR code below:

System of Government Questions

13. Name <u>one</u> branch or part of the government.*

14. What stops <u>one</u> branch of government from becoming too powerful?

15. Who is in charge of the executive branch?

16. Who makes federal laws?

17. What are the <u>two</u> parts of the U.S. Congress?*

18. How many U.S. Senators are there?

19. We elect a U.S. Senator for how many years?

20. Who is <u>one</u> of your state's U.S. Senators now?*

21. The House of Representatives has how many voting members?

22. We elect a U.S. Representative for how many years?

23. Name your U.S. Representative.

24. Who does a U.S. Senator represent?

25. Why do some states have more Representatives than other states?

26. We elect a President for how many years?

27. In what month do we vote for President?*

28. What is the name of the President of the United States now?*

29. What is the name of the Vice President of the United States now?

30. If the President can no longer serve, who becomes President?

31. If both the President and the Vice President can no longer serve, who becomes President?

32. Who is the Commander in Chief of the military?

33. Who signs bills to become laws?

34. Who vetoes bills?

35. What does the President's Cabinet do?

36. What are <u>two</u> Cabinet-level positions?

37. What does the judicial branch do?

38. What is the highest court in the United States?

39. How many justices are on the Supreme Court?

40. Who is the Chief Justice of the United States now?

41. Under our Constitution, some powers belong to the federal government. What is <u>one</u> power of the federal government?

42. Under our Constitution, some powers belong to the states. What is <u>one</u> power of the states?

43. Who is the Governor of your state now?

44. What is the capital of your state?*

45. What are the <u>two</u> major political parties in the United States?*

46. What is the political party of the President now?

47. What is the name of the Speaker of the House of Representatives now?

Answers

13. Name <u>one</u> branch or part of the government.*
    - Congress
    - legislative
    - President
    - executive
    - the courts
    - judicial

14. What stops <u>one</u> branch of government from becoming too powerful?
    - checks and balances
    - separation of powers

15. Who is in charge of the executive branch?
    - the President

16. Who makes federal laws?
    - Congress
    - Senate and House (of Representatives)
    - (U.S. or national) legislature

17. What are the <u>two</u> parts of the U.S. Congress?*
    - the Senate and House (of Representatives)

18. How many U.S. Senators are there?
    - one hundred (100)

19. We elect a U.S. Senator for how many years?
    - six (6)

20. Who is <u>one</u> of your state's U.S. Senators now?*
    - Answers will vary. Go here to find yours: studyguideteam.com/civics

21. The House of Representatives has how many voting members?
    - four hundred thirty-five (435)

22. We elect a U.S. Representative for how many years?
    - two (2)

23. Name your U.S. Representative.
    - Answers will vary. Go here to find yours: studyguideteam.com/civics

24. Who does a U.S. Senator represent?
    - all people of the state

25. Why do some states have more Representatives than other states?
    - (because of) the state's population
    - (because) they have more people
    - (because) some states have more people

26. We elect a President for how many years?
    - four (4)

27. In what month do we vote for President?*
    - November

28. What is the name of the President of the United States now?*
    - Joseph R. Biden, Jr.
    - Joe Biden
    - Biden

    This can change. Visit studyguideteam.com/civics for the latest information.

29. What is the name of the Vice President of the United States now?
- Kamala D. Harris
- Kamala Harris
- Harris

This can change. Visit studyguideteam.com/civics for the latest information.

30. If the President can no longer serve, who becomes President?
- the Vice President

31. If both the President and the Vice President can no longer serve, who becomes President?
- the Speaker of the House

32. Who is the Commander in Chief of the military?
- the President

33. Who signs bills to become laws?
- the President

34. Who vetoes bills?
- the President

35. What does the President's Cabinet do?
- advises the President

36. What are two Cabinet-level positions?
- Secretary of Agriculture
- Secretary of Commerce
- Secretary of Defense
- Secretary of Education
- Secretary of Energy
- Secretary of Health and Human Services
- Secretary of Homeland Security
- Secretary of Housing and Urban Development
- Secretary of the Interior
- Secretary of Labor

- Secretary of State
- Secretary of Transportation
- Secretary of the Treasury
- Secretary of Veterans Affairs
- Attorney General
- Vice President

37. What does the judicial branch do?
- reviews laws
- explains laws
- resolves disputes (disagreements)
- decides if a law goes against the Constitution

38. What is the highest court in the United States?
- the Supreme Court

39. How many justices are on the Supreme Court?
- Nine (9)

This can change. Visit studyguideteam.com/civics for the latest information.

40. Who is the Chief Justice of the United States now?
- John Roberts
- John G. Roberts, Jr.

This can change. Visit studyguideteam.com/civics for the latest information.

41. Under our Constitution, some powers belong to the federal government. What is <u>one</u> power of the federal government?
- to print money
- to declare war
- to create an army
- to make treaties

42. Under our Constitution, some powers belong to the states. What is one power of the states?
- provide schooling and education
- provide protection (police)
- provide safety (fire departments)
- give a driver's license
- approve zoning and land use

43. Who is the Governor of your state now?
- Answers will vary. Go here to find yours: studyguideteam.com/civics

44. What is the capital of your state?*
- Answers will vary. Go here to find yours: studyguideteam.com/civics

44. What is the capital of your state?*
- Answers will vary. Go here to find yours: studyguideteam.com/civics or use the table below:

State	Capital	State	Capital
Alabama	Montgomery	Iowa	Des Moines
Alaska	Juneau	Kansas	Topeka
Arizona	Phoenix	Kentucky	Frankfort
Arkansas	Little Rock	Louisiana	Baton Rouge
California	Sacramento	Maine	Augusta
Colorado	Denver	Maryland	Annapolis
Connecticut	Hartford	Massachusetts	Boston
Delaware	Dover	Michigan	Lansing
Florida	Tallahassee	Minnesota	Saint Paul
Georgia	Atlanta	Mississippi	Jackson
Hawaii	Honolulu	Missouri	Jefferson City
Idaho	Boise	Montana	Helena
Illinois	Springfield	Nebraska	Lincoln
Indiana	Indianapolis	Nevada	Carson City

State	Capital		State	Capital
New Hampshire	Concord		South Carolina	Columbia
New Jersey	Trenton		South Dakota	Pierre
New Mexico	Santa Fe		Tennessee	Nashville
New York	Albany		Texas	Austin
North Carolina	Raleigh		Utah	Salt Lake City
North Dakota	Bismarck		Vermont	Montpelier
Ohio	Columbus		Virginia	Richmond
Oklahoma	Oklahoma City		Washington	Olympia
Oregon	Salem		West Virginia	Charleston
Pennsylvania	Harrisburg		Wisconsin	Madison
Rhode Island	Providence		Wyoming	Cheyenne

[District of Columbia residents should answer that D.C. is not a state and does not have a capital. Residents of U.S. territories should name the capital of the territory.]

45. What are the two major political parties in the United States?*
   • Democratic and Republican

46. What is the political party of the President now?
   • Democratic (party)

This can change. Visit studyguideteam.com/civics for the latest information.

47. What is the name of the Speaker of the House of Representatives now?
   • Nancy Pelosi
   • Pelosi

This can change. Visit studyguideteam.com/civics for the latest information.

Rights and Responsibilities

Freedoms

Voting
One of the most important freedoms that U.S. citizens have is the right to vote. There are four amendments in the Constitution that explain who has the right to vote:

- The Fifteenth Amendment gave African-American men the right to vote.

- The Nineteenth Amendment gave women the right to vote.

- The Twenty-Fourth Amendment eliminated poll taxes.

- The Twenty-Sixth Amendment lowered the voting age to 18.

Bill of Rights
The Bill of Rights gives everyone living in the United States certain rights. These include the freedom of speech, freedom of expression, freedom to petition the government, freedom of assembly, freedom of religion, and the right to bear arms.

Public Service

Democracy
There are multiple ways in which Americans can participate in democracy, including voting, joining a political party, writing to a newspaper, running for office, giving an elected official your opinion on an issue, joining a civic group, helping with a campaign, calling Senators and Representatives, or publicly supporting or opposing an issue.

There are some responsibilities and rights that are reserved only for U.S. citizens. Some of these responsibilities include serving on a jury and voting in federal elections. Some of these rights include the opportunities to vote in a federal election and run for federal office.

This means that only U.S. citizens can run for Congress or the presidency.

One important way that citizens can honor and show loyalty to the United States and its flag is by reciting the **Pledge of Allegiance**. This pledge is significant and it is meant to be recited while holding your right hand over your heart and looking directly at the flag. The Pledge of Allegiance was originally written by Francis Bellamy in August of 1892, though the pledge has undergone some changes since then. Today it reads:

> "I pledge allegiance to the flag of the United States of America, and to the republic for which it stands, one nation under God, indivisible, with liberty and justice for all."

Government

When becoming a United States citizen, you make the promise to give up loyalty to other countries and swear loyalty only the United States. You also make the promise to defend and obey the Constitution and the laws of the country, serve in the U.S. military if needed, and perform other important work for the nation when necessary. Because of this, all men must register for the **Selective Service** between the ages of **18** and **26**.

All U.S. citizens have an obligation and responsibility to pay taxes to the government. Each year, citizens must file their annual income tax returns. **April 15th** is the last day that citizens can send in federal income tax forms.

Rights and Responsibilities Questions

48. There are four amendments to the Constitution about who can vote. Describe <u>one</u> of them.

49. What is <u>one</u> responsibility that is only for United States citizens?*

50. Name <u>one</u> right only for United States citizens.

51. What are <u>two</u> rights of everyone living in the United States?

52. What do we show loyalty to when we say the Pledge of Allegiance?

53. What is <u>one</u> promise you make when you become a United States citizen?

54. How old do citizens have to be to vote for President?*

55. What are <u>two</u> ways that Americans can participate in their democracy?

56. When is the last day you can send in federal income tax forms?*

57. When must all men register for the Selective Service?

Answers

48. There are four amendments to the Constitution about who can vote. Describe one of them.
   - Citizens eighteen (18) and older (can vote).
   - You don't have to pay (a poll tax) to vote.
   - Any citizen can vote. (Women and men can vote.)
   - A male citizen of any race (can vote).

49. What is one responsibility that is only for United States citizens?*
   - serve on a jury
   - vote in a federal election

50. Name one right only for United States citizens.
   - vote in a federal election
   - run for federal office

51. What are two rights of everyone living in the United States?
   - freedom of expression
   - freedom of speech
   - freedom of assembly
   - freedom to petition the government
   - freedom of religion
   - the right to bear arms

52. What do we show loyalty to when we say the Pledge of Allegiance?
   - the United States
   - the flag

53. What is one promise you make when you become a United States citizen?
   - give up loyalty to other countries
   - defend the Constitution and laws of the United States
   - obey the laws of the United States
   - serve in the U.S. military (if needed)

- serve (do important work for) the nation (if needed)
- be loyal to the United States

54. How old do citizens have to be to vote for President?*
- eighteen (18) and older

55. What are <u>two</u> ways that Americans can participate in their democracy?
- vote
- join a political party
- help with a campaign
- join a civic group
- join a community group
- give an elected official your opinion on an issue
- call Senators and Representatives
- publicly support or oppose an issue or policy
- run for office
- write to a newspaper

56. When is the last day you can send in federal income tax forms?*
- April 15

57. When must all men register for the Selective Service?
- at age eighteen (18)
- between eighteen (18) and twenty-six (26)

Colonial Period and Independence

The Union

Colonization

In the year 1620, Puritan settlers sailed to North America on a ship called the *Mayflower*. These Puritans, also known as Pilgrims, left England in pursuit of religious freedom, political liberty, and economic opportunity. Two months after they set sail, the Pilgrims landed at Plymouth Rock, where they signed the Mayflower Compact, creating the first official government. The Puritans, led by William Bradford, began befriending the **Native Americans**—also referred to as **American Indians**—who had been living in America long before the Europeans arrived. Some of the most well-known Native Americans whom the Puritans befriended were Squanto and chief Massasoit.

Slavery

During the 17th and 18th centuries, native **Africans** were taken from their homes and sold as slaves in the Americas. As a cheaper alternative to paid servants, these men, women, and children were used for labor in the production of crops such as cotton and tobacco. The first African slaves in America were brought to Jamestown, Virginia, in 1619. The moral problem of slavery was the central reason behind the American Civil War, which was fought between the United States (the North) and the Confederacy (the South). The institution of slavery existed in the United States until President Abraham Lincoln abolished it through the 13th Amendment in 1865.

States

By 1732, the United States was comprised of thirteen colonies: Virginia, New York, Massachusetts, Connecticut, New Hampshire, Maryland, Delaware, Rhode Island, Pennsylvania, New Jersey, North Carolina, South Carolina, and Georgia. These states were all colonies of the British

Empire, but as they grew increasingly independent over the years, tensions began to rise.

This tension between American colonists and British officials began during the French and Indian War. Because of the war, the British Crown obtained a hefty amount of expenses, which led to higher taxes for the colonies. These high taxes, along with the unjust quartering of British soldiers in American homes, became the tipping point for the colonists. Incidents such as the Boston Massacre and the Boston Tea Party continued to further the divide between the colonists and the British. Since they had no government of their own, the colonists plotted to overthrow their oppressors and pursue their own independence.

On April 19, 1775, colonial soldiers, also known as minutemen, fired on British troops at Lexington and Concord. This battle officially began the American Revolution. The war lasted for seven long years until the British finally surrendered at the Battle of Yorktown. The Treaty of Paris was signed on September 3, 1783, signifying Great Britain's acknowledgment of America's independence.

Important Documents

Declaration of Independence
The Declaration of Independence is one of the most important documents in American history. It was written primarily by **Thomas Jefferson** and was adopted on **July 4, 1776**. This document was America's declaration against the rule of the British Crown.

The Constitution
On **May 14, 1787**, fifty-five men met in Philadelphia, Pennsylvania, in order to establish how the newly formed nation would be governed. This meeting was known as the **Constitutional Convention,** and it lasted until September 17, 1787. During this convention, the Founding Fathers revised the already existing Articles of Confederation and formed the current **Constitution**, which governs the United States to this day.

The Federalist Papers

The Federalist Papers, previously known as *The Federalist*, are a collection of eighty-five essays and articles that sought to encourage voters to ratify the Constitution. Written by Alexander **Hamilton**, James **Madison**, and John **Jay** under the group pseudonym of "**Publius**," the Federalist Papers explained the Constitution in detail and sought to encourage voters to adopt it over the Articles of Confederation.

Founding Fathers

Members

The men who structured the United States' government and served as its early leaders are known as the **Founding Fathers**. The most well-known and influential of these men include George Washington, Benjamin Franklin, Thomas Jefferson, John Adams, James Madison, Alexander Hamilton, and James Monroe. George Washington was the Commander in Chief of the Continental Army during the American Revolution and also served as the first president of the newly formed nation. John Adams, Thomas Jefferson, James Madison, and James Monroe also served as presidents.

Alexander Hamilton served as the first Secretary of the U.S. Treasury. **Benjamin Franklin** was a man of many talents, as he served as a U.S. diplomat, started the first free libraries, wrote the famous book *Poor Richard's Almanac*, served as the first U.S. Postmaster General, and was the oldest member of the Constitutional Convention.

Presidents

There have been forty-six presidents who have served throughout America's history, with **George Washington** being the first. Because of this fact, along with his other immense contributions to the United States' foundation, Washington is considered the "**Father of Our Country**". Both a state and the capital of our nation are named after him. Washington served as president from 1789 to 1797.

Colonial Period and Independence Questions

58. What is <u>one</u> reason colonists came to America?

59. Who lived in America before the Europeans arrived?

60. What group of people was taken to America and sold as slaves?

61. Why did the colonists fight the British?

62. Who wrote the Declaration of Independence?

63. When was the Declaration of Independence adopted?

64. There were 13 original states. Name <u>three</u>.

65. What happened at the Constitutional Convention?

66. When was the Constitution written?

67. The Federalist Papers supported the passage of the U.S. Constitution. Name <u>one</u> of the writers.

68. What is <u>one</u> thing Benjamin Franklin is famous for?

69. Who is the "Father of Our Country"?

70. Who was the first President?*

Answers

58. What is <u>one</u> reason colonists came to America?
    - freedom
    - political liberty
    - religious freedom
    - economic opportunity
    - practice their religion
    - escape persecution

59. Who lived in America before the Europeans arrived?
    - American Indians
    - Native Americans

60. What group of people was taken to America and sold as slaves?
    - Africans
    - people from Africa

61. Why did the colonists fight the British?
    - because of high taxes (taxation without representation)
    - because the British army stayed in their houses (boarding, quartering)
    - because they didn't have self-government

62. Who wrote the Declaration of Independence?
    - (Thomas) Jefferson

63. When was the Declaration of Independence adopted?
    - July 4, 1776

64. There were 13 original states. Name <u>three</u>.
    - New Hampshire
    - Massachusetts
    - Rhode Island
    - Connecticut
    - New York
    - New Jersey

- Pennsylvania
- Delaware
- Maryland
- Virginia
- North Carolina
- South Carolina
- Georgia

65. What happened at the Constitutional Convention?
   - The Constitution was written.
   - The Founding Fathers wrote the Constitution.

66. When was the Constitution written?
   - 1787

67. *The Federalist Papers* supported the passage of the U.S. Constitution. Name <u>one</u> of the writers.
   - (James) Madison
   - (Alexander) Hamilton
   - (John) Jay
   - Publius

68. What is <u>one</u> thing Benjamin Franklin is famous for?
   - U.S. diplomat
   - oldest member of the Constitutional Convention
   - first Postmaster General of the United States
   - writer of *Poor Richard's Almanac*
   - started the first free libraries

69. Who is the "Father of Our Country"?
   - (George) Washington

70. Who was the first President?*
   - (George) Washington

1800s

Major Events

International Events

The **1800s**, also known as the **19th century**, brought about momentous growth and change for the United States. It saw the rise of democracy, industrialism, and labor movements. It saw the discovery of new lands and gave birth to new ideologies and businesses. It also brought about devasting difficulties from war, slavery, and poverty. From the purchase of the French territory of **Louisiana** in 1803 to the rise of the cowboy in the American West in the 1870s, the 19th century was a truly defining century in America's history.

Wars

War has been an inevitable occurrence throughout history, and the 19th century saw the U.S. fighting in four different wars: the War of 1812, the Mexican-American War, the Civil War, and the Spanish-American War.

The **War of 1812**, also known as the Second War of Independence, was fought between the U.S. and Great Britain from June of 1812 to February of 1815. The war was fought over maritime rights, Great Britain's impressment of American sailors, and Great Britain's encouragement of Native American violence against U.S. citizens.

The **Mexican-American War** was fought between the U.S. and Mexico from April of 1846 to February of 1848. The war was fought over western territory and Mexico's disapproval of the annexation of Texas.

The **American Civil War**—also referred to as the War Between the States—pitted Americans against one another: Union soldiers in the North versus Confederate soldiers in the South. This war was fought from April of 1861 to April of 1865, and it was fought over **economic issues, states' rights**, and the issue of **slavery**.

The **Spanish-American War** was a conflict between Spain and the United States, who supported Cuban independence from Spanish rule. A treaty, with terms more favorable for the U.S., ended the conflict as well as the last of Spanish control in the Caribbean.

Abolition

Abolitionism, also known as the abolitionist movement, was the organized effort to dismantle the institution of slavery in the United States. Abolitionism first emerged in the 1830s and ended with the signing of the **Emancipation Proclamation** in 1863. The proclamation was declared halfway through the Civil War, and it changed the meaning of the war entirely. No longer was the war focused just on preserving the Union; it was about abolishing slavery. This proclamation freed the slaves throughout the United States, including in the Confederate states.

Important Figures

Presidents

From Thomas Jefferson to William McKinley, twenty-two men served as president throughout the 19th century.

Perhaps the most well-known of the 19th century presidents is Abraham Lincoln, the man who led the nation through the Civil War from 1861-1865. Lincoln issued the Emancipation Proclamation, which freed the slaves, led the nation through the Civil War, and preserved the Union. The Lincoln Memorial in Washington, D.C., was erected in his honor.

Citizens

The 19th century held no shortages of memorable and influential citizens. People such as Clara Barton, Thomas Edison, Mark Twain, and Susan B. Anthony were authors, inventors, and civil rights activists who changed the course of society in the United States. Clara Barton was a nurse who founded the American Red Cross. Thomas Edison is known for inventing incredible devices, such as the motion picture camera, the phonograph, and the incandescent light bulb. Mark Twain, whose real name was Samuel Clemens, was an author and lecturer who is known as the "Father of American Literature." **Susan B. Anthony** was a women's rights activist who fought for the civil rights of women and African-Americans.

1800s Questions

71. What territory did the United States buy from France in 1803?

72. Name <u>one</u> war fought by the United States in the 1800s.

73. Name the U.S. war between the North and the South.

74. Name <u>one</u> problem that led to the Civil War.

75. What was <u>one</u> important thing that Abraham Lincoln did?*

76. What did the Emancipation Proclamation do?

77. What did Susan B. Anthony do?

Answers

71. What territory did the United States buy from France in 1803?
    - the Louisiana Territory
    - Louisiana

72. Name <u>one</u> war fought by the United States in the 1800s.
    - War of 1812
    - Mexican-American War
    - Civil War
    - Spanish-American War

73. Name the U.S. war between the North and the South.
    - the Civil War
    - the War between the States

74. Name <u>one</u> problem that led to the Civil War.
    - slavery
    - economic reasons
    - states' rights

75. What was <u>one</u> important thing that Abraham Lincoln did?*
    - freed the slaves (Emancipation Proclamation)
    - saved (or preserved) the Union
    - led the United States during the Civil War

76. What did the Emancipation Proclamation do?
    - freed the slaves
    - freed slaves in the Confederacy
    - freed slaves in the Confederate states
    - freed slaves in most Southern states

77. What did Susan B. Anthony do?
    - fought for women's rights
    - fought for civil rights

Recent American History and Other Important Historical Information

Wars

The **1900s**, which made up the **20th century**, were filled with war. The United States fought in five wars throughout the century, two of which were worldwide conflicts. The five wars were World War I, World War II, the Korean War, the Vietnam War, and the Persian Gulf War.

World War I, also known as the Great War, saw the United States, Great Britain, France, Russia, Italy, Romania, and Japan (the Allied Powers) fight against Germany, Austria-Hungary, Bulgaria, and the Ottoman Empire (the Central Powers). The war began when a Serbian nationalist assassinated Austrian Archduke Franz Ferdinand. From there, countries all over Europe and Asia took sides in the massive conflict. After the war ended, **President Woodrow Wilson**, who led the United States during the war, sought to create a League of Nations that would prevent a global war from ever happening again. This did not succeed, however, as the first World War led directly to the second.

World War II saw the United States, Great Britain, France, and the Soviet Union (Allied Powers) fight against **Japan, Germany, and Italy** (Axis Powers). This war began when Adolf Hitler, leader of the Nazi Party and Germany, invaded Poland in 1939. From there, countries all over the world picked sides. **President Franklin D. Roosevelt** led the nation through the Great Depression to the end of the second World War. A few famous American generals who served in the war were George S. Patton, Douglas MacArthur, and **Dwight Eisenhower**, who eventually became president.

The **Korean War** and **Vietnam War** were the physical conflicts that manifested from the overarching conflict known as the **Cold War**. The

Cold War was fought to overcome the rise of **communism**, which was spreading through and to nations and territories such as the Soviet Union, North Korea, Vietnam, East Germany, and Poland. The Cold War lasted from the late 40s to the early 90s.

The **Persian Gulf War** was fought in the Middle East from August of 1990 to February of 1991. It saw the United States leading thirty-four different nations against Iraq, led by Iraqi president Saddam Hussein who had invaded Kuwait over oil production conflicts.

Civil Right

The 1950s and 1960s saw the rise of the **civil rights** movement, a social justice movement with the goal of gaining lawful, equal rights for Black Americans and ending the racial discrimination that had persisted since the Civil War. Rosa Parks helped begin the civil rights movement by refusing to give up her seat to a white man on a public bus. **Martin Luther King, Jr.** was a minister who worked for civil rights and for the equality of Black Americans. He became the most well-known leader in the civil rights movement, and his famous "I Have a Dream" speech was both televised and heard on the radio around the nation.

Terrorism

On **September 11, 2001**, radical Islamic jihadists hijacked four airline jets. They crashed two of them into the World Trade Center towers in New York City and one into the Pentagon in Washington, D.C. Due to the heroic actions of passengers onboard, the fourth plane crashed in a field rather than into a building as originally plotted. Nearly 3,000 people were killed in these attacks. These were the first major terrorist attacks to occur on American soil, and they directly triggered American mobilization to combat terrorism in the Middle East.

American Indian Tribes

The 20th century saw much needed change for American Indian tribes in the form of the Indian Reorganization Act. This act sought to encourage and strengthen American Indians' traditional culture, rather than forcing them to assimilate to American traditions. While some government officials continued to pressure tribes into assimilating to American culture, more reforms were made through the Native American civil rights movement, which helped increase awareness of the struggles that the tribes endured. Native tribes such as the Cherokee, Sioux, Pueblo, Choctaw, Navajo, and Chippewa all sought to gain respect from the U.S. government and its citizens.

Recent American History & Other Important Historical Information Questions

78. Name <u>one</u> war fought by the United States in the 1900s.*

79. Who was President during World War I?

80. Who was President during the Great Depression and World War II?

81. Who did the United States fight in World War II?

82. Before he was President, Eisenhower was a general. What war was he in?

83. During the Cold War, what was the main concern of the United States?

84. What movement tried to end racial discrimination?

85. What did Martin Luther King, Jr. do?*

86. What major event happened on September 11, 2001, in the United States?

87. Name <u>one</u> American Indian tribe in the United States. [USCIS Officers will be supplied with a list of federally recognized American Indian tribes.]

Answers

78. Name <u>one</u> war fought by the United States in the 1900s.*
    - World War I
    - World War II
    - Korean War
    - Vietnam War
    - (Persian) Gulf War

79. Who was President during World War I?
    - (Woodrow) Wilson

80. Who was President during the Great Depression and World War II?
    - (Franklin) Roosevelt

81. Who did the United States fight in World War II?
    - Japan, Germany, and Italy

82. Before he was President, Eisenhower was a general. What war was he in?
    - World War II

83. During the Cold War, what was the main concern of the United States?
    - Communism

84. What movement tried to end racial discrimination?
    - civil rights (movement)

85. What did Martin Luther King, Jr. do?*
    - fought for civil rights
    - worked for equality for all Americans

86. What major event happened on September 11, 2001, in the United States?
    - Terrorists attacked the United States.

87. Name <u>one</u> American Indian tribe in the United States. [USCIS Officers will be supplied with a list of federally recognized American Indian tribes.]

- Cherokee
- Navajo
- Sioux
- Chippewa
- Choctaw
- Pueblo
- Apache
- Iroquois
- Creek
- Blackfeet
- Seminole
- Cheyenne
- Arawak
- Shawnee
- Mohegan
- Huron
- Oneida
- Lakota
- Crow
- Teton
- Hopi
- Inuit

Geography

Bodies of Water

Rivers
The United States has over 250,000 rivers flowing through its territory. The longest river in the nation is the **Missouri River**, a 2,341-mile-long river that flows from Three Forks, Montana, to St. Louis, Missouri. The second longest river is the 2,318-mile-long **Mississippi River**, which flows from northern Minnesota all the way to Louisiana, where it empties into the Gulf of Mexico.

Coasts
There are three primary coasts in the United States: the Pacific Coast, the Atlantic Coast, and the Gulf Coast. The **Pacific Ocean** lies on America's West Coast, the **Atlantic Ocean** lies on the East Coast, and the **Gulf of Mexico** lies on the Gulf Coast.

States and Cities

U.S. Territories
The U.S. has five different territories that can be found in Pacific Ocean and Caribbean Sea. They are:

- Puerto Rico
- U.S. Virgin Islands
- American Samoa
- Northern Mariana Islands
- Guam

Two countries border the United States: Mexico and Canada. The states that border Mexico are Texas, New Mexico, Arizona, and California. The states that share a land border with Canada are Maine, Vermont, New York, New Hampshire, Minnesota, Michigan, Idaho, Montana, North Dakota, Washington, and Alaska. In addition, Ohio and Pennsylvania share a water border with Canada through Lake Erie.

Capitals

Each state within the U.S. has its own capital city, but the capital city of the nation is **Washington, D.C.** Examples of other capitals in the country are Austin (Texas), Sacramento (California), Tallahassee (Florida), and Albany (New York).

Monuments

There are one hundred and twenty-nine national monuments in the U.S. Some include the Grand Canyon in Arizona, The Devil's Tower in Wyoming, and the **Statue of Liberty**, which stands on Liberty Island in New York Harbor.

Geography Questions

88. Name <u>one</u> of the two longest rivers in the United States.

89. What ocean is on the West Coast of the United States?

90. What ocean is on the East Coast of the United States?

91. Name <u>one</u> U.S. territory.

92. Name <u>one</u> state that borders Canada.

93. Name <u>one</u> state that borders Mexico.

94. What is the capital of the United States?*

95. Where is the Statue of Liberty?*

Answers

88. Name <u>one</u> of the two longest rivers in the United States.
    - Missouri (River)
    - Mississippi (River)

89. What ocean is on the West Coast of the United States?
    - Pacific (Ocean)

90. What ocean is on the East Coast of the United States?
    - Atlantic (Ocean)

91. Name <u>one</u> U.S. territory.
    - Puerto Rico
    - U.S. Virgin Islands
    - American Samoa
    - Northern Mariana Islands
    - Guam

92. Name <u>one</u> state that borders Canada.
    - Maine
    - New Hampshire
    - Vermont
    - New York
    - Pennsylvania
    - Ohio
    - Michigan
    - Minnesota
    - North Dakota
    - Montana
    - Idaho
    - Washington
    - Alaska

93. Name <u>one</u> state that borders Mexico.
- California
- Arizona
- New Mexico
- Texas

94. What is the capital of the United States?*
- Washington, D.C.

95. Where is the Statue of Liberty?*
- New York (Harbor)
- Liberty Island

[Also acceptable are New Jersey, near New York City, and on the Hudson (River).]

Symbols

American Flag

On June 14, 1777, the Continental Congress requested that an official flag be made for the newly founded United States of America. Nicknamed "Old Glory," the flag is said to have been designed by Congressman Francis Hopkins and sewn by Betsy Ross, a seamstress from Pennsylvania. The original flag had thirteen stars and thirteen stripes. Over the next one hundred and eighty-three years, the flag went through numerous changes in its design. The current design was adopted in 1960 after the annexation of Hawaii.

Stripes
There are thirteen stripes on the American flag, each representing one of the original thirteen colonies. The color red represents valor, and white represents purity.

Stars
There are fifty stars on the American flag, each representing one of the fifty states within the union. The color blue behind the stars represents vigilance and justice.

National Anthem

On September 14, 1814, Francis Scott Key wrote "**The Star-Spangled Banner.**" Key wrote the poem after witnessing Fort McHenry being attacked by the British during the War of 1812. Though the poem has four stanzas, only the first is sung as the national anthem. "The Star-Spangled Banner" was officially adopted as the national anthem on March 3, 1931.

The anthem is as follows:

> O say can you see, by the dawn's early light,
>
> What so proudly we hailed at the twilight's last gleaming,

Whose broad stripes and bright stars through the perilous fight,

O'er the ramparts we watched, were so gallantly streaming?

And the rocket's red glare, the bombs bursting in air,

Gave proof through the night that our flag was still there;

O say does that star-spangled banner yet wave

O'er the land of the free and the home of the brave?

Symbols Questions

96. Why does the flag have 13 stripes?

97. Why does the flag have 50 stars?*

98. What is the name of the national anthem?

Answers

96. Why does the flag have 13 stripes?
    - because there were 13 original colonies
    - because the stripes represent the original colonies

97. Why does the flag have 50 stars?*
    - because there is one star for each state
    - because each star represents a state
    - because there are 50 states

98. What is the name of the national anthem?
    - The Star-Spangled Banner

Holidays

Independence Day

The Fourth of July, also known as Independence Day, is a national holiday that celebrates America's independence from Great Britain. Since the Declaration of Independence was adopted on July 4, 1776, this national holiday is celebrated every year on **July 4th**.

Other National Holidays

There are many other holidays celebrated in the United States. The national holidays in the U.S. are:

Holiday	Observed
New Year's Day	January 1st
Martin Luther King, Jr. Day	Third Monday in January
Presidents' Day	Third Monday in February
Memorial Day	Last Monday in May
Juneteenth	June 19th
Independence Day	July 4th
Labor Day	First Monday in September
Columbus Day	Second Monday in October
Veterans Day	November 11th
Thanksgiving Day	Fourth Thursday in November
Christmas	December 25th

Holidays Questions

99. When do we celebrate Independence Day?*

100. Name <u>two</u> national U.S. holidays.

Answers

99. When do we celebrate Independence Day?*
   - July 4

100. Name <u>two</u> national U.S. holidays.
   - New Year's Day
   - Martin Luther King, Jr. Day
   - Presidents' Day
   - Memorial Day
   - Juneteenth
   - Independence Day
   - Labor Day
   - Columbus Day
   - Veterans Day
   - Thanksgiving
   - Christmas

Full Practice Test

1. What is the supreme law of the land?

2. What does the Constitution do?

3. The idea of self-government is in the first three words of the Constitution. What are these words?

4. What is an amendment?

5. What do we call the first ten amendments to the Constitution?

6. What is <u>one</u> right or freedom from the First Amendment?*

7. How many amendments does the Constitution have?

8. What did the Declaration of Independence do?

9. What are <u>two</u> rights in the Declaration of Independence?

10. What is freedom of religion?

11. What is the economic system in the United States?*

12. What is the "rule of law"?

13. Name <u>one</u> branch or part of the government.*

14. What stops <u>one</u> branch of government from becoming too powerful?

15. Who is in charge of the executive branch?

16. Who makes federal laws?

17. What are the <u>two</u> parts of the U.S. Congress?*

18. How many U.S. Senators are there?

19. We elect a U.S. Senator for how many years?

20. Who is <u>one</u> of your state's U.S. Senators now?*

21. The House of Representatives has how many voting members?

22. We elect a U.S. Representative for how many years?

23. Name your U.S. Representative.

24. Who does a U.S. Senator represent?

25. Why do some states have more Representatives than other states?

26. We elect a President for how many years?

27. In what month do we vote for President?*

28. What is the name of the President of the United States now?*

29. What is the name of the Vice President of the United States now?

30. If the President can no longer serve, who becomes President?

31. If both the President and the Vice President can no longer serve, who becomes President?

32. Who is the Commander in Chief of the military?

33. Who signs bills to become laws?

34. Who vetoes bills?

35. What does the President's Cabinet do?

36. What are <u>two</u> Cabinet-level positions?

37. What does the judicial branch do?

38. What is the highest court in the United States?

39. How many justices are on the Supreme Court?

40. Who is the Chief Justice of the United States now?

41. Under our Constitution, some powers belong to the federal government. What is <u>one</u> power of the federal government?

42. Under our Constitution, some powers belong to the states. What is <u>one</u> power of the states?

43. Who is the Governor of your state now?

44. What is the capital of your state?*

45. What are the <u>two</u> major political parties in the United States?*

46. What is the political party of the President now?

47. What is the name of the Speaker of the House of Representatives now?

48. There are four amendments to the Constitution about who can vote. Describe one of them.

49. What is one responsibility that is only for United States citizens?*

50. Name one right only for United States citizens.

51. What are two rights of everyone living in the United States?

52. What do we show loyalty to when we say the Pledge of Allegiance?

53. What is one promise you make when you become a United States citizen?

54. How old do citizens have to be to vote for President?*

55. What are two ways that Americans can participate in their democracy?

56. When is the last day you can send in federal income tax forms?*

57. When must all men register for the Selective Service?

58. What is one reason colonists came to America?

59. Who lived in America before the Europeans arrived?

60. What group of people was taken to America and sold as slaves?

61. Why did the colonists fight the British?

62. Who wrote the Declaration of Independence?

63. When was the Declaration of Independence adopted?

64. There were 13 original states. Name three.

65. What happened at the Constitutional Convention?

66. When was the Constitution written?

67. The Federalist Papers supported the passage of the U.S. Constitution. Name one of the writers.

68. What is one thing Benjamin Franklin is famous for?

69. Who is the "Father of Our Country"?

70. Who was the first President?*

71. What territory did the United States buy from France in 1803?

72. Name one war fought by the United States in the 1800s.

73. Name the U.S. war between the North and the South.

74. Name one problem that led to the Civil War.

75. What was one important thing that Abraham Lincoln did?*

76. What did the Emancipation Proclamation do?

77. What did Susan B. Anthony do?

78. Name one war fought by the United States in the 1900s.*

79. Who was President during World War I?

80. Who was President during the Great Depression and World War II?

81. Who did the United States fight in World War II?

82. Before he was President, Eisenhower was a general. What war was he in?

83. During the Cold War, what was the main concern of the United States?

84. What movement tried to end racial discrimination?

85. What did Martin Luther King, Jr. do?*

86. What major event happened on September 11, 2001, in the United States?

87. Name one American Indian tribe in the United States. [USCIS Officers will be supplied with a list of federally recognized American Indian tribes.]

88. Name one of the two longest rivers in the United States.

89. What ocean is on the West Coast of the United States?

90. What ocean is on the East Coast of the United States?

91. Name <u>one</u> U.S. territory.

92. Name <u>one</u> state that borders Canada.

93. Name <u>one</u> state that borders Mexico.

94. What is the capital of the United States?*

95. Where is the Statue of Liberty?*

96. Why does the flag have 13 stripes?

97. Why does the flag have 50 stars?*

98. What is the name of the national anthem?

99. When do we celebrate Independence Day?*

100. Name <u>two</u> national U.S. holidays.

Full Answer Key

1. What is the supreme law of the land?
   - the Constitution

2. What does the Constitution do?
   - sets up the government
   - defines the government
   - protects basic rights of Americans

3. The idea of self-government is in the first three words of the Constitution. What are these words?
   - We the People

4. What is an amendment?
   - a change (to the Constitution)
   - an addition (to the Constitution)

5. What do we call the first ten amendments to the Constitution?
   - the Bill of Rights

6. What is <u>one</u> right or freedom from the First Amendment?*
   - speech
   - religion
   - assembly
   - press
   - petition the government

7. How many amendments does the Constitution have?
   - twenty-seven (27)

8. What did the Declaration of Independence do?
   - announced our independence (from Great Britain)
   - declared our independence (from Great Britain)
   - said that the United States is free (from Great Britain)

9. What are <u>two</u> rights in the Declaration of Independence?
- life
- liberty
- pursuit of happiness

10. What is freedom of religion?
- You can practice any religion, or not practice a religion.

11. What is the economic system in the United States?*
- capitalist economy
- market economy

12. What is the "rule of law"?
- Everyone must follow the law.
- Leaders must obey the law.
- Government must obey the law.
- No one is above the law.

13. Name <u>one</u> branch or part of the government.*
- Congress
- legislative
- President
- executive
- the courts
- judicial

14. What stops <u>one</u> branch of government from becoming too powerful?
- checks and balances
- separation of powers

15. Who is in charge of the executive branch?
- the President

16. Who makes federal laws?
- Congress
- Senate and House (of Representatives)
- (U.S. or national) legislature

17. What are the <u>two</u> parts of the U.S. Congress?*
    - the Senate and House (of Representatives)

18. How many U.S. Senators are there?
    - one hundred (100)

19. We elect a U.S. Senator for how many years?
    - six (6)

20. Who is <u>one</u> of your state's U.S. Senators now?*
    - Answers will vary. Go here to find yours:
      studyguideteam.com/civics

21. The House of Representatives has how many voting members?
    - four hundred thirty-five (435)

22. We elect a U.S. Representative for how many years?
    - two (2)

23. Name your U.S. Representative.
    - Answers will vary. Go here to find yours:
      studyguideteam.com/civics

24. Who does a U.S. Senator represent?
    - all people of the state

25. Why do some states have more Representatives than other states?
    - (because of) the state's population
    - (because) they have more people
    - (because) some states have more people

26. We elect a President for how many years?
    - four (4)

27. In what month do we vote for President?*
    - November

28. What is the name of the President of the United States now?*
- Joseph R. Biden, Jr.
- Joe Biden
- Biden

This can change. Visit studyguideteam.com/civics for the latest information.

29. What is the name of the Vice President of the United States now?
- Kamala D. Harris
- Kamala Harris
- Harris

This can change. Visit studyguideteam.com/civics for the latest information.

30. If the President can no longer serve, who becomes President?
- the Vice President

31. If both the President and the Vice President can no longer serve, who becomes President?
- the Speaker of the House

32. Who is the Commander in Chief of the military?
- the President

33. Who signs bills to become laws?
- the President

34. Who vetoes bills?
- the President

35. What does the President's Cabinet do?
- advises the President

36. What are <u>two</u> Cabinet-level positions?
- Secretary of Agriculture
- Secretary of Commerce
- Secretary of Defense
- Secretary of Education
- Secretary of Energy
- Secretary of Health and Human Services
- Secretary of Homeland Security
- Secretary of Housing and Urban Development
- Secretary of the Interior
- Secretary of Labor
- Secretary of State
- Secretary of Transportation
- Secretary of the Treasury
- Secretary of Veterans Affairs
- Attorney General
- Vice President

37. What does the judicial branch do?
- reviews laws
- explains laws
- resolves disputes (disagreements)
- decides if a law goes against the Constitution

38. What is the highest court in the United States?
- the Supreme Court

39. How many justices are on the Supreme Court?
- Nine (9)

This can change. Visit studyguideteam.com/civics for the latest information.

40. Who is the Chief Justice of the United States now?
- John Roberts
- John G. Roberts, Jr.

This can change. Visit studyguideteam.com/civics for the latest information.

41. Under our Constitution, some powers belong to the federal government. What is <u>one</u> power of the federal government?
- to print money
- to declare war
- to create an army
- to make treaties

42. Under our Constitution, some powers belong to the states. What is <u>one</u> power of the states?
- provide schooling and education
- provide protection (police)
- provide safety (fire departments)
- give a driver's license
- approve zoning and land use

43. Who is the Governor of your state now?
- Answers will vary. Go here to find yours: studyguideteam.com/civics

44. What is the capital of your state?*
   - Answers will vary. Go here to find yours: studyguideteam.com/civics or use the table below:

State	Capital	State	Capital
Alabama	Montgomery	Montana	Helena
Alaska	Juneau	Nebraska	Lincoln
Arizona	Phoenix	Nevada	Carson City
Arkansas	Little Rock	New Hampshire	Concord
California	Sacramento	New Jersey	Trenton
Colorado	Denver	New Mexico	Santa Fe
Connecticut	Hartford	New York	Albany
Delaware	Dover	North Carolina	Raleigh
Florida	Tallahassee	North Dakota	Bismarck
Georgia	Atlanta	Ohio	Columbus
Hawaii	Honolulu	Oklahoma	Oklahoma City
Idaho	Boise	Oregon	Salem
Illinois	Springfield	Pennsylvania	Harrisburg
Indiana	Indianapolis	Rhode Island	Providence
Iowa	Des Moines	South Carolina	Columbia
Kansas	Topeka	South Dakota	Pierre
Kentucky	Frankfort	Tennessee	Nashville
Louisiana	Baton Rouge	Texas	Austin
Maine	Augusta	Utah	Salt Lake City
Maryland	Annapolis	Vermont	Montpelier
Massachusetts	Boston	Virginia	Richmond
Michigan	Lansing	Washington	Olympia
Minnesota	Saint Paul	West Virginia	Charleston
Mississippi	Jackson	Wisconsin	Madison
Missouri	Jefferson City	Wyoming	Cheyenne

[District of Columbia residents should answer that D.C. is not a state and does not have a capital. Residents of U.S. territories should name the capital of the territory.]

45. What are the <u>two</u> major political parties in the United States?*
- Democratic and Republican

46. What is the political party of the President now?
- Democratic (party)

This can change. Visit uscis.gov/citizenship/testupdates for the latest information.

47. What is the name of the Speaker of the House of Representatives now?
- Nancy Pelosi
- Pelosi

Visit uscis.gov/citizenship/testupdates for the name of the Speaker of the House of Representatives.

48. There are four amendments to the Constitution about who can vote. Describe <u>one</u> of them.
- Citizens eighteen (18) and older (can vote).
- You don't have to pay (a poll tax) to vote.
- Any citizen can vote. (Women and men can vote.)
- A male citizen of any race (can vote).

49. What is <u>one</u> responsibility that is only for United States citizens?*
- serve on a jury
- vote in a federal election

50. Name <u>one</u> right only for United States citizens.
- vote in a federal election
- run for federal office

51. What are <u>two</u> rights of everyone living in the United States?
- freedom of expression

- freedom of speech
- freedom of assembly
- freedom to petition the government
- freedom of religion
- the right to bear arms

52. What do we show loyalty to when we say the Pledge of Allegiance?
- the United States
- the flag

53. What is <u>one</u> promise you make when you become a United States citizen?
- give up loyalty to other countries
- defend the Constitution and laws of the United States
- obey the laws of the United States
- serve in the U.S. military (if needed)
- serve (do important work for) the nation (if needed)
- be loyal to the United States

54. How old do citizens have to be to vote for President?*
- eighteen (18) and older

55. What are <u>two</u> ways that Americans can participate in their democracy?
- vote
- join a political party
- help with a campaign
- join a civic group
- join a community group
- give an elected official your opinion on an issue
- call Senators and Representatives
- publicly support or oppose an issue or policy
- run for office
- write to a newspaper

56. When is the last day you can send in federal income tax forms?*
- April 15

57. When must all men register for the Selective Service?
- at age eighteen (18)
- between eighteen (18) and twenty-six (26)

58. What is <u>one</u> reason colonists came to America?
- freedom
- political liberty
- religious freedom
- economic opportunity
- practice their religion
- escape persecution

59. Who lived in America before the Europeans arrived?
- American Indians
- Native Americans

60. What group of people was taken to America and sold as slaves?
- Africans
- people from Africa

61. Why did the colonists fight the British?
- because of high taxes (taxation without representation)
- because the British army stayed in their houses (boarding, quartering)
- because they didn't have self-government

62. Who wrote the Declaration of Independence?
- (Thomas) Jefferson

63. When was the Declaration of Independence adopted?
- July 4, 1776

64. There were 13 original states. Name <u>three</u>.
- New Hampshire
- Massachusetts
- Rhode Island
- Connecticut
- New York

- New Jersey
- Pennsylvania
- Delaware
- Maryland
- Virginia
- North Carolina
- South Carolina
- Georgia

65. What happened at the Constitutional Convention?
- The Constitution was written.
- The Founding Fathers wrote the Constitution.

66. When was the Constitution written?
- 1787

67. The Federalist Papers supported the passage of the U.S. Constitution. Name <u>one</u> of the writers.
- (James) Madison
- (Alexander) Hamilton
- (John) Jay
- Publius

68. What is <u>one</u> thing Benjamin Franklin is famous for?
- U.S. diplomat
- oldest member of the Constitutional Convention
- first Postmaster General of the United States
- writer of *Poor Richard's Almanac*
- started the first free libraries

69. Who is the "Father of Our Country"?
- (George) Washington

70. Who was the first President?*
- (George) Washington

71. What territory did the United States buy from France in 1803?
- the Louisiana Territory
- Louisiana

72. Name <u>one</u> war fought by the United States in the 1800s.
- War of 1812
- Mexican-American War
- Civil War
- Spanish-American War

73. Name the U.S. war between the North and the South.
- the Civil War
- the War between the States

74. Name <u>one</u> problem that led to the Civil War.
- slavery
- economic reasons
- states' rights

75. What was <u>one</u> important thing that Abraham Lincoln did?*
- freed the slaves (Emancipation Proclamation)
- saved (or preserved) the Union
- led the United States during the Civil War

76. What did the Emancipation Proclamation do?
- freed the slaves
- freed slaves in the Confederacy
- freed slaves in the Confederate states
- freed slaves in most Southern states

77. What did Susan B. Anthony do?
- fought for women's rights
- fought for civil rights

78. Name <u>one</u> war fought by the United States in the 1900s.*
- World War I
- World War II
- Korean War

- Vietnam War
- (Persian) Gulf War

79. Who was President during World War I?
- (Woodrow) Wilson

80. Who was President during the Great Depression and World War II?
- (Franklin) Roosevelt

81. Who did the United States fight in World War II?
- Japan, Germany, and Italy

82. Before he was President, Eisenhower was a general. What war was he in?
- World War II

83. During the Cold War, what was the main concern of the United States?
- Communism

84. What movement tried to end racial discrimination?
- civil rights (movement)

85. What did Martin Luther King, Jr. do?*
- fought for civil rights
- worked for equality for all Americans

86. What major event happened on September 11, 2001, in the United States?
- Terrorists attacked the United States.

87. Name one American Indian tribe in the United States. [USCIS Officers will be supplied with a list of federally recognized American Indian tribes.]
- Cherokee
- Navajo
- Sioux
- Chippewa
- Choctaw

- Pueblo
- Apache
- Iroquois
- Creek
- Blackfeet
- Seminole
- Cheyenne
- Arawak
- Shawnee
- Mohegan
- Huron
- Oneida
- Lakota
- Crow
- Teton
- Hopi
- Inuit

88. Name <u>one</u> of the two longest rivers in the United States.
- Missouri (River)
- Mississippi (River)

89. What ocean is on the West Coast of the United States?
- Pacific (Ocean)

90. What ocean is on the East Coast of the United States?
- Atlantic (Ocean)

91. Name <u>one</u> U.S. territory.
- Puerto Rico
- U.S. Virgin Islands
- American Samoa
- Northern Mariana Islands
- Guam

92. Name <u>one</u> state that borders Canada.
- Maine
- New Hampshire
- Vermont
- New York
- Pennsylvania
- Ohio
- Michigan
- Minnesota
- North Dakota
- Montana
- Idaho
- Washington
- Alaska

93. Name <u>one</u> state that borders Mexico.
- California
- Arizona
- New Mexico
- Texas

94. What is the capital of the United States?*
- Washington, D.C.

95. Where is the Statue of Liberty?*
- New York (Harbor)
- Liberty Island

[Also acceptable are New Jersey, near New York City, and on the Hudson (River).]

96. Why does the flag have 13 stripes?
- because there were 13 original colonies
- because the stripes represent the original colonies

97. Why does the flag have 50 stars?*
- because there is one star for each state
- because each star represents a state
- because there are 50 states

98. What is the name of the national anthem?
- The Star-Spangled Banner

99. When do we celebrate Independence Day?*
- July 4

100. Name <u>two</u> national U.S. holidays.
- New Year's Day
- Martin Luther King, Jr. Day
- Presidents' Day
- Memorial Day
- Independence Day
- Labor Day
- Columbus Day
- Veterans Day
- Thanksgiving
- Christmas

Simulated Test #1

Questions

1. What is the supreme law of the land?

2. What is the economic system in the United States?*

3. What did the Emancipation Proclamation do?

4. When was the Declaration of Independence adopted?

5. Who was the first President?*

6. When must all men register for the Selective Service?

7. What do we show loyalty to when we say the Pledge of Allegiance?

8. What is <u>one</u> responsibility that is only for United States citizens?*

9. Who does a U.S. Senator represent?

10. What is the political party of the President now?

Answers

1. What is the supreme law of the land?
   - the Constitution

2. What is the economic system in the United States?*
   - capitalist economy
   - market economy

3. What did the Emancipation Proclamation do?
   - freed the slaves
   - freed slaves in the Confederacy
   - freed slaves in the Confederate states
   - freed slaves in most Southern states

4. When was the Declaration of Independence adopted?
   - July 4, 1776

5. Who was the first President?*
   - (George) Washington

6. When must all men register for the Selective Service?
   - at age eighteen (18)
   - between eighteen (18) and twenty-six (26)

7. What do we show loyalty to when we say the Pledge of Allegiance?
   - the United States
   - the flag

8. What is one responsibility that is only for United States citizens?*
   - serve on a jury
   - vote in a federal election

9. Who does a U.S. Senator represent?
   - all people of the state

10. What is the political party of the President now?
- Democratic (party)

This can change. Visit studyguideteam.com/civics for the latest information.

Simulated Test #2

Questions

1. What are <u>two</u> rights in the Declaration of Independence?

2. In what month do we vote for President?*

3. When is the last day you can send in federal income tax forms?*

4. What was <u>one</u> important thing that Abraham Lincoln did?*

5. What movement tried to end racial discrimination?

6. Name <u>one</u> war fought by the United States in the 1900s.*

7. Name <u>one</u> U.S. territory.

8. Name <u>one</u> of the two longest rivers in the United States.

9. Why does the flag have 50 stars?*

10. Who makes federal laws?

Answers

1. What are <u>two</u> rights in the Declaration of Independence?
   - life
   - liberty
   - pursuit of happiness

2. In what month do we vote for President?*
   - November

3. When is the last day you can send in federal income tax forms?*
   - April 15

4. What was <u>one</u> important thing that Abraham Lincoln did?*
   - freed the slaves (Emancipation Proclamation)
   - saved (or preserved) the Union
   - led the United States during the Civil War

5. What movement tried to end racial discrimination?
   - civil rights (movement)

6. Name <u>one</u> war fought by the United States in the 1900s.*
   - World War I
   - World War II
   - Korean War
   - Vietnam War
   - (Persian) Gulf War

7. Name <u>one</u> U.S. territory.
   - Puerto Rico

8. Name <u>one</u> of the two longest rivers in the United States.
   - Missouri (River)
   - Mississippi (River)

9. Why does the flag have 50 stars?*
- because there is one star for each state
- because each star represents a state
- because there are 50 states

10. Who makes federal laws?
- Congress
- Senate and House (of Representatives)
- (U.S. or national) legislature

Simulated Test #3

Questions

1. Why do some states have more Representatives than other states?

2. Who is in charge of the executive branch?

3. What did Susan B. Anthony do?

4. During the Cold War, what was the main concern of the United States?

5. What is the name of the national anthem?

6. What major event happened on September 11, 2001, in the United States?

7. What ocean is on the East Coast of the United States?

8. Who is the Commander in Chief of the military?

9. When do we celebrate Independence Day?*

10. What is an amendment?

Answers

1. Why do some states have more Representatives than other states?
   - (because of) the state's population
   - (because) they have more people
   - (because) some states have more people

2. Who is in charge of the executive branch?
   - the President

3. What did Susan B. Anthony do?
   - fought for women's rights
   - fought for civil rights

4. During the Cold War, what was the main concern of the United States?
   - Communism

5. What is the name of the national anthem?
   - The Star-Spangled Banner

6. What major event happened on September 11, 2001, in the United States?
   - Terrorists attacked the United States.

7. What ocean is on the East Coast of the United States?
   - Atlantic (Ocean)

8. Who is the Commander in Chief of the military?
   - the President

9. When do we celebrate Independence Day?*
   - July 4

10. What is an amendment?
    - a change (to the Constitution)
    - an addition (to the Constitution)

CPSIA information can be obtained
at www.ICGtesting.com
Printed in the USA
LVHW020755161122
733125LV00015B/411

9 781637 754214